# The Love of Oliver

By Gay Haines

Illustrated by Trudi Gilliam

ISBN # 978-0-578-91087-1
Printed in USA

I would like to dedicate this book to every child who believes in the healing love a dog can give, and in particular to the Suncoast Humane Society and the Child Protection Center who, through their Pet Therapy Programs provide that opportunity.

Lily

Merry 1ST Christmas!

This book was first read
to your great-grandmother
in November. Enjoy the
story as much as she did!

Love  GAS & GUS

2021

After I passed the "good dog" test, I earned a vest that had my name on it! Little did I know then how that green vest would change my life for the next ten years. Oh, I had a job alright and no two days would ever be the same.

Perhaps it was around my second birthday, as close as I remember, I went to Suncoast Humane Society and passed my interview. I was young, obeyed my mom, and got along well with everybody, but my mom told me that I needed to go help other people.... and that's pretty much how my story began.

I had no idea how many kids went to school so I could help them learn to read, and then they would go to the library to read to me! As many kids as I saw, who read with me, I never got tired of hearing the same story over and over again. Sometimes they would turn their book around to show me the pictures. I liked that part the best.

Once I was an honor guard at church! It was a funeral for a lady who loved dogs and wanted me, and ten of my friends, to be there for her family. There was a German Shepard, Golden Retriever, a medium sized Schnauzer, and several others that were a mix of many other dogs. It was a sad day, but the people were happy to see me. A choir played hymns on big loud bells, and I never even barked! Afterwards, my dog friends and I got bones and biscuits. Kinda cool.

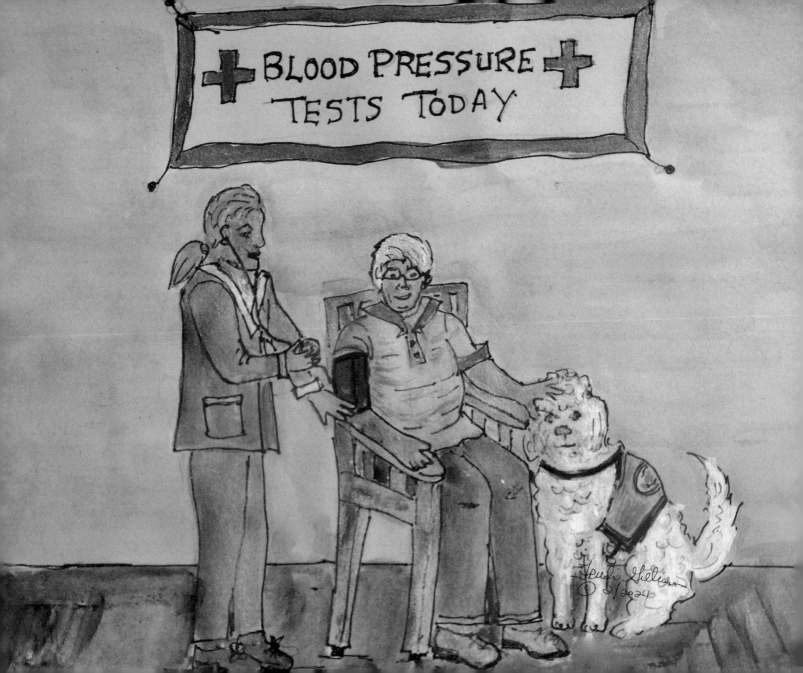

I went to a Health Fair for people. Other dogs were helping out too. I got to sit with a man while a nurse took his blood pressure which was very high. The man talked to me for a while, petted me, then a nurse took his pressure again and it was much lower. I got credit for being a good dog that day! Maybe I helped with a miracle!

I spent at least one day a week visiting with old people. Really old. They were in chairs with wheels on them, but they would pet me and that made them smile. How simple was that! Other days we would go to nursing homes and rehab places. That was nice to help people get better and feel better and make them less lonely.

I was able to visit people who weren't feeling well and had to stay in bed. Some were in hospitals and others were in nursing homes or places where seniors stay. They were always so happy to see me because they told me stories about their dogs. Some people wanted me to get up on their bed with them. I'm not big enough, but I was able to get close enough for them to pet me and ask me to come back to visit them again very soon. They were nice people.

I did go to a high school, when something sad happened; some students and a teacher had died. I went to sit with these big kids who just wanted to hug me, and cry a bit. My mom was sad that day, and I was helpful to her as well. I was getting used to helping people, even my mom. Making people feel better was the best part of my job.

A courthouse is a big building. Inside are many workers who have come to help. There are sheriffs, secretaries, legal people and they all call me by name and want to say hello to me and thank me for coming. I have to go through security to get inside, but it's ok, I don't mind a bit.

Courtrooms can be scary for kids, but if I'm with them listening to them tell their stories to a judge, or an attorney, they feel better and more safe. I would come home pretty tired, but I knew I helped them get through their bad day.

That's what I do. I help people. Old and young. Big and small. I often get to work with lots of my dog friends. All my dog friends look different from me, just like all the people we help. It is the best job ever and I love being a therapy dog.

**M**y name is Oliver, and I hope to see you around somewhere. I'll be the one with apricot colored curls and I'll be wearing my green vest with my name on it.

I'll be looking out for you... just in case you need my help.

I would like to send a special woof-out to some dedicated friends who have also helped many children along the way: Abbey, Bentley, Brooke, Buck, Crackers, Daisy, Django, Fiona-Marie, Hercules, Jaeger, Raven, Ruby-Begonia, Shaggy, Stella, and so many more furry friends. A very big bark for Claire Berten and Danielle Hughes of Suncoast Humane Society and Child Protection Center who have been excellent leaders of their pack.

My mom would like to thank Chris Goodier, James Knake, Sherrie Isle, and in particular, Trudi Gilliam who has captured my features and situations so wonderfully. All these good people have been very helpful along the way.

After all, dogs can't be expected to do everything!